ANIMAL SAFARI

Camels

by Megan Borgert-Spaniol

BELLWETHER MEDIA • MINNEAPOLIS, MN

Note to Librarians, Teachers, and Parents:

Blastoff! Readers are carefully developed by literacy experts and combine standards-based content with developmentally appropriate text.

Level 1 provides the most support through repetition of high-frequency words, light text, predictable sentence patterns, and strong visual support.

Level 2 offers early readers a bit more challenge through varied simple sentences, increased text load, and less repetition of high-frequency words.

Level 3 advances early-fluent readers toward fluency through increased text and concept load, less reliance on visuals, longer sentences, and more literary language.

Level 4 builds reading stamina by providing more text per page, increased use of punctuation, greater variation in sentence patterns, and increasingly challenging vocabulary.

Level 5 encourages children to move from "learning to read" to "reading to learn" by providing even more text, varied writing styles, and less familiar topics.

Whichever book is right for your reader, Blastoff! Readers are the perfect books to build confidence and encourage a love of reading that will last a lifetime!

Contents

What Are Camels?

Camels are **mammals** with one or two humps on their backs.

Desert Living

They live in
dry **deserts**.
These lands
can be very
hot or cold.

Thick coats keep camels warm in the winter. They **shed** to stay cool in the summer.

Camels have bushy eyebrows and long eyelashes. This protects their eyes from sand and ice.

Large, round feet help camels walk on top of sand and snow.

Camels have tough lips and mouths. This lets them eat plants with **thorns**.

Camel Humps

Camels store fat in their humps. They use the fat when there is no food or water around.

Camels can live for
weeks without water.
They can live for
months without food.

A camel's hump gets floppy when the fat is gone. This camel is hungry!

Glossary

deserts—dry lands with little rain; very few plants and animals live in deserts.

mammals—warm-blooded animals that have backbones and feed their young milk

shed—to get rid of the outer layer of hair

thorns—the sharp parts of some plants

To Learn More

AT THE LIBRARY

Forties, Justine. *How the Camel Got Its Hump: Tales from Around the World.* New York, N.Y.: Golden Books, 2001.

Ganeri, Anita. *Bactrian Camel.* Chicago, Ill.: Heinemann Library, 2011.

Peet, Bill. *Pamela Camel.* Boston, Mass.: Houghton Mifflin, 1984.

ON THE WEB

Learning more about camels is as easy as 1, 2, 3.

1. Go to www.factsurfer.com

2. Enter "camels" in the search box.

3. Click the Surf button and you will see a list of related Web sites.

With factsurfer.com, finding more information is just a click away.

Index